English

The Straightforward English series is designed to measure, teach, review, and master specific English writing skills.

Capitalization
and
Punctuation

by S. Harold Collins

Cover design by Kathy Kifer

GarlicPress

www.garlicpress.com

Our mission is to provide you with the best materials available to aid in the education of learners of any age.

Published by:
Garlic Press
605 Powers St.
Eugene, OR 97402

ISBN: 978-0-931993-32-9
Order Number GP-032
Printed in China

www.garlicpress.com

Straight Forward English Series

Dear Parents and Teachers,

The **Straight Forward English Series** has been designed for parents, teachers, and students. The Series is composed of books designed to measure, teach, review, and master specific English skills. The focus of this book is capitalization and punctuation.

What makes this series different?

- These are the capitalization and punctuation skills essential to the mastery of English structure and form.

- This series reflects national standards crucial to mastery of capitalization and punctuation.

- Capitalization and punctuation skills are concisely explained, practiced, and tested.

- Mastery can be measured by comparing the Beginning Assessment Test with the Final Assessment Test.

- More content. No distracting or unrelated pictures or words. The skills are straightforward.

How to use this book:

- Give the Beginning Assessment Test to gain a starting measure of a student's verb skills.

- Progress through each topic. Work the exercises. Exercise work can be done in the book or on a separate sheet of paper. Set a standard to move from one topic to the next. If the standard is not met, go back and refocus on that topic.

- Give the Final Assessment Test to gain an ending measure of a student's capitalization and punctuation skills. Compare the Beginning Assessment Test and Final Assessment Test as a reflection of skill acquisition.

Contents

Beginning Assessment Test

A. Capitalization, Abbreviation, and Ending Marks. Rewrite each sentence. Use capital letters. Punctuate abbreviations. Use the correct ending marks.

1. will you come with me to the founder's day parade

2. he and i will meet you there

3. the boy asked emily and elena for a ride

4. don't do that

5. does dr linda l smith live here

6. We went to florida in june to see disney world

7. Our leader said, "stop "

8. The first american president was george washington

9. Next tuesday at 3:00 P M , we will arrive in canada

10. He said, "tomorrow is valentine's day "

11. I am not sure if i called mrs d c alexis

12. Did you include our trip to oregon and crater lake

B. Commas. Rewrite each sentence. Place commas correctly.

1. Today is Wednesday July 6 1990.

2. I went to the store and she went home.

3. Mr. Moore our teacher called my parents last night.

4. Yes we will fly to Oakland California.

5. John spoke quietly "They left their hats coats and towels here."

6. Please take care of our dogs cats and parrot.

7. Thank you Marie for your map of Denver Colorado.

8. I like it but it is not my favorite.

9. "It's closer than you think" remarked Juan.

10. By the way the letter was mailed May 3 1946 by my uncle.

11. Gold red green and blue are the favorite colors of Jane Alice and Bill.

12. Only four people Jill can go with Becky.

13. How old is Barko your dog?

14. Together they shouted "Look out!"

15. He held the pole and she attached the sign.

Beginning Assessment Test

C. Apostrophes. Form a contraction for each pair of words.

1. I would _____

2. you are _____

3. do not _____

4. they had _____

5. they have _____

6. could not _____

7. she had _____

8. we have _____

9. I will _____

10. he is _____

11. could have _____

12. should not _____

D. Possessives. Rewrite each phrase, forming the correct possessive.

1. Mary name _____

2. one child game _____

3. four children game _____

4. the Jones yard _____

5. several stores signs _____

6. many dogs collars _____

7. Ms. Lopez house _____

8. both nurses smiles _____

9. J.B. Doris car _____

10. the spider web _____

11. two days work _____

12. New Year Day _____

Capitalization

  1 and First Words

 Capitalize the word I wherever it appears.

EXAMPLES: May I go with you?
He said you and I may go.
I will leave soon.

> Capitalize the first word in a sentence.

EXAMPLES: It is ten days until Christmas.
Let's drive to the next city to shop.
Rake the leaves into a pile.

> Capitalize the first word in a direct quotation.

EXAMPLES: "My name is Arthur," he said.
She answered, "My name is Maria."
"How long," he asked, "have you been here?"

Exercise 1. Capitalize I, all first words in a sentence, and all first words in direct quotations.

1. the morning was clear and brisk.

2. they awoke before their parents did.

3. "i'm glad we came on this camping trip," said Elena.

4. her brother replied, "it has been more than i expected."

5. "are you two awake?" came their father's voice.

6. eric answered, "we just woke up."

7. after breakfast, the family decided to go for a hike.

8. "the trail begins over here, i think," said his father.

9. they walked to the trailhead.

10. pointing to the sign, Elena said, "i think we should take this trail."

11. they all agreed.

12. "we can have lunch at the lake," said her father.

13. "yes, but i also want to go for a swim," added Eric.

14. their father said, "before we go, be sure to take your lunch and swimsuit."

15. both children answered together, "we will.

Capitalization

 CHAPTER **Proper Nouns**

> Proper Nouns are nouns that name a particular person, place, or thing.

People's Names and Titles (some examples)

First Names: Jane, Stan, Emily
Full Names: Maria Alicia DeSoto, Bill Moore, Jr.
Initials in Names: William I. Moore, Maria A. DeSoto
Names with Titles: Mrs. Smith, President Lincoln, Mayor Alberta Mills

Exercise 1. Capitalize all proper nouns.

1. On our visit to the state capitol, we met governor evans.
2. Sue and james are brother and sister.
3. The sign read, "mrs. felicia r. jerome, m.d."
4. We met senator garcia, too.
5. One neighbor is t. b. goodyear, and the other is captain mary lutz.
6. Have you seen albert l. riveria, sr., or mr. and mrs. thorn?
7. Who is the president of the club?
8. Ambassador warren introduced us to the other ambassadors.
9. The lottery was won by j. michael chang and his sister, jane.
10. The principal of our school is mrs. virginia daniels.
11. The first prize was presented to my uncle leon.
12. My sister and grandmother went shopping.
13. My friend marsha has a puppy that she named miles.
14. The order is for john, marie, terry, gail, and max.
15. Their aunt and uncle finally met miss green.

Particular Places (some examples)

Cities: New York, Calgary, Fargo
States: Oregon, North Dakota, Kansas
Countries: United States, Canada, China, India
Geographic Features: Mt. Everest, Pacific Ocean, Lake Erie
Geographic Regions: Europe, Asia, Africa, Pacific Northwest
Streets: Elm St., 4th Av., Hillview Lane
Parks: Yellowstone National Park, Banff National Park

Exercise 2. Capitalize all proper places.

1. The andes mountains are in chile and argentina.

2. Which is larger, los angeles, california, or denver, colorado?

3. Lake placid is in new york.

4. The mississippi river flows from minnesota to the gulf of mexico.

5. The store is at the corner of park lane and coburg road.

6. You might need a reservation to stay in yosemite national park.

7. The smallest state is rhode island.

8. Drive home by way of oak grove, golden valley, and murphy.

9. Canada, the united states, and mexico are part of north america.

10. The lewis and clark expedition reached the pacific ocean in 1803.

11. We went backpacking in the rocky mountains.

12. The hawaiian islands are not in the atlantic ocean.

13. The green mountains are in vermont.

14. Deliver this to 246 west andover street.

15. Alberta, british columbia, and manitoba are provinces in canada.

Particular Things (some examples)

Days, holidays, months: Tuesday, July 4th, January
Special events: World War I, Civil War, Summer Celebration
Organizations, businesses, stores: Sierra Club, Salvation Army,
    International Airlines, Red Cross
Nationalities: German, Chinese
Brand names: Big Mac, Campbell's Soup, Ivory Soap

Exercise 3. Capitalize all proper things.

1. We are to meet you on wednesday, march 3, in omaha, nebraska.

2. This year, christmas falls on sunday.

3. The irish like to celebrate st. patrick's day.

4. How many months are between may and december?

5. The card shop is open on thursday.

6. The world car association holds its yearly meeting in april.

7. Let's stop and get a big mac.

8. I already know what I will be for halloween.

9. The portland chamber of commerce has a parade every labor day.

10. The bank of montreal is open until 5:00 P.M. monday through friday.

11. The american lung association has a special event each year.

12. The french settled here before the turn of the century.

13. John's father works for lane county health department.

14. Buy a quart of carnation's milk and a case of coca-cola.

15. How many cards do you need for valentine's day?

16. The american civil war was fought between 1861 and 1865.

17. The native american dancers will perform during the festival of lights.

18. My membership in the sierra club expires in december.

19. That club meets every other week.

20. Did you donate blood to the red cross?

Exercise 4. Capitalize all proper nouns.

Have I told you about milton johnston? He is my uncle. We visit him every year at easter. We drive to kalispell, montana, to see him. He lives on the south end of main street, across the street from the rocky mountain museum.

Sometimes we go to flathead lake and fish. And sometimes we visit glacier national park or waterton glacier international peace park. The waterton glacier international peace park crosses the united states and canada border and extends into the province of alberta.

When we go to either park, we cross the continental divide. We have visited the town of st. mary. We have also visited the nearby blackfoot indian reservation.

My uncle milton tells us stories. He tells us about working for the great northern railroad. And he tells us about meeting famous people. He once met charles russell, the painter.

CHAPTER 3 Ending Marks and Sentences

 The **period** is used to end a declarative sentence. A *declarative sentence* makes a statement. It tells us something.

EXAMPLES: It is raining.
The airplane landed on time.
Our cat is gray and white.
School is closed next week.

 The **period** is also used to end an imperative sentence. An *Imperative sentence* commands or directs you to do something.

EXAMPLES: Please lock the door.
Don't forget your coat.
Put the book away.
Bring me the other one.

 The **period** is also used with abbreviations. Common abbreviations are used for days of the week, months, titles, and initials.

EXAMPLES:

Tuesday—Tues.	Street—St.	before noon—A.M.
Monday—Mon.	Avenue—Av.	before Christ—B.C.
January—Jan.	A.C. Smith, Jr.	Elena Collins, M.D.
Doctor—Dr.	Ann R. Green	Mistress—Mrs.
week—wk.		

 The **question mark** is used at the end of an interrogatory sentence. An *interrogatory sentence* asks something.

EXAMPLES: What time is it?
Do you think it will stop raining?
Where are you going?
Would you close the door?

The **exclamation mark** is used to end an exclamatory sentence. An *exclamatory sentence* shows strong feeling or surprise.

EXAMPLES: What a beautiful coat!
Stop! Don't do that!
Ouch, that hurt!
I can't believe you did that!

Exercise 1. Read each sentence. Add the correct ending mark and write **Decl.**, **Imper.**, **Inter.**, or **Excl.** after each sentence.

1. Can you remember the color

2. Put the books on the shelf

3. Look at that accident

4. The bus left them behind

5. Please don't forget to lock the door

6. Did you lock the door

7. What a fine new car

8. The sun is setting over the hills

9. Would you take this to my home

10. The next town is only a few miles away

Exercise 2. Read each sentence. Add the correct ending mark. Add periods to any abbreviations.

The morning was cold   Dr Ann Moore and her husband, J B Moore, drove along Would it snow   They wondered   It was 9:30 A M when they arrived at the cabin

J B got out of the car   Did he have a key to the cabin   Was 110 Center St the correct address   He asked Ann   It was

"What a beautiful cabin " exclaimed Ann   The long drive from Albany, Calif , had been worth it   They would stay until Wed morning

Review 1: Capitalization & Punctuation

Read the following story. Correct all capitalization errors. Some words shouldn't be capitalized. Place correct ending marks on sentences.

I have a friend   his name is charles smoot, but I call him chuck

Chuck lives in the willamette valley of oregon   have you ever heard of eugene oregon eugene is his hometown

Chuck goes to Washington school   he plays many School sports and belongs to several School Clubs

Chuck and I met through the mail   his teacher and mine started a writing exchange between students   Chuck wrote to me first, and then I answered Or was it the other way around

Chuck has told me that he has a Sister named ellen   His mother, who works at the university of oregon, is a University teacher   His father is President of a small business called lane county lumber

Chuck does many things with his family in the Winter   they can downhill ski at mt. bachelor, or they can cross country ski anywhere near the three Sisters wilderness area

The nearby cascade mountains are beautiful   the smoots can hike or camp in the summer   they don't have to travel far

this summer, I will travel across canada and the united states to stay with the smoots   I will travel either by greyhound bus or united airlines I will be there in august   Doesn't that sound exciting

 **Commas: Dates and Addresses**

CHAPTER 4

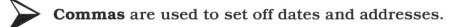 **Commas** are used to set off dates and addresses.

Commas and Dates

EXAMPLES: Tuesday, January 11
July 4, 1776
The baby was born on May 2, 1968, in the morning.

In sentences: A comma is needed before and after the year when the month and day are given.

EXAMPLE: March 12, 1972, was our first family reunion.

In sentences: A comma is not needed when only the month and year are stated.

EXAMPLE: March 1992 was our first family reunion.

Commas and Addresses

EXAMPLES: Charlottesville, Virginia
Toronto, Ontario
Her home at 7 North Main St., Denver, Colorado, is not far.

In sentences: A comma is needed before and after a state or country when the name of the city is stated.

EXAMPLE: Seattle, Washington, is north of Portland, Oregon.

Exercise I. Place commas correctly.

1. Tuesday June 29
2. September 1 1928
3. Montreal Quebec
4. Sunday April 24 1988
5. New York City New York
6. March 14 1945
7. Paris France
8. Seattle Washington
9. Mexico City Mexico
10. Friday July 9
11. San Francisco California
12. Saturday August 23
13. London England
14. October 13 1985
15. Wednesday May 19 1988
16. Atlanta Georgia
17. September 11 1960
18. St. Louis Missouri
19. Saturday November 22
20. March 24 1782

Exercise 2. Place commas correctly.

1. Today's date is January 11 1988.

2. The last day of the year is Tuesday December 31.

3. Why is July 4 1776 such an important date?

4. Address the letter to 23 First Av. Portland Oregon.

5. How far is it from Rome Italy to Moscow Russia?

6. On Tuesday September 10 1976 she will be fourteen.

7. The business was founded June 1 1924 in Ottawa Ontario.

8. He was born in Newton Vermont but moved to San Diego California.

9. Toronto Ontario is not far from Buffalo New York.

10. The offlce on 1246 Hillview is open until Friday August 2.

Exercise 3. Place commas in the following headings.

1. 45 Taft St.
   Minneapolis Minnesota 55413
   December 31 1948

2. 999 South Jason St.
   Saint John New Brunswick E2K 2A9
   November 22 1911

3. 62 North 47th Av.
   Glendale Arizona 85301
   October 31 1977

4. 8593 College Av.
   Ft. Meyers Florida 33919
   January 11 1997

5. 6561 Beach St.
   Buena Park California 90621
   February 30 2007

6. 460 Horner Av.
   Toronto Ontario M8W 4X2
   March 12 2008

Exercise 4. Place commas where they are needed.

1. They arrived here in March 1989.

2. Send this letter to Mexico City Mexico before next week.

3. The letter was sent May 12 1990 and arrived three days later.

4. You can drive from Toronto Ontario to Montreal Quebec in one day.

5. The event took place in September of 1912.

6. Deliver this to 127 Maple St. Springfield Oregon by tomorrow.

7. Los Angeles California is nearly an eight hour drive from Phoenix Arizona.

8. January 11 1946 is my birth date.

9. He flew from Ontario Canada to Seattle Washington.

10. The letter was postmarked Panama City Panama on November 22 1911.

 # Commas: Introductory Words
and Nouns of Address

 Introductory Words. Use a comma to set off single words like *yes,* *no,* or *well* when they introduce a sentence.

EXAMPLES: Yes, I will answer the phone.
Well, the door was closed.
No, you had better try again.

The comma after an introducing word indicates a slight pause.

Introductory words can also be **short phrases** like: *of course, by the way,* or *first of all.*

EXAMPLES: By the way, did you get an answer?
Of course, I may never know what really happened.
First of all, you must return the hammer.

Nouns of Address. Use commas to set off the names of people to whom you are speaking or writing.

EXAMPLES: Emily, please put those away.
The letters were mailed yesterday, Mr. Gomez.
Thank you, Jane, for returning the book.

Nouns of address can be set off by one comma or by two commas. Use one comma for a noun of address at the beginning or at the end of a sentence. Use two commas if the noun of address is in the middle of a sentence.

Exercise I. Use commas to set off nouns of address. You will need 13 commas.

1. Did you call me Mr. Stein?

2. Lee make sure the door is shut.

3. Please Sara watch what you are doing.

4. Give this to John Bill.

5. Robert what is the date tomorrow?

6. Thank you Susan for remembering to get the cake.

7. Scott please help Syd with the dinner.

8. Mr. and Mrs. Rovetta here is your table.

9. I believe sir you are wrong.

10. We are going home first Emily.

Exercise 2. Use commas to set off the introductory words or phrases in the following sentences.

1. Yes you have been successful!
2. By the way how far is it?
3. Well my brother will help me.
4. No you must first complete the assignment.
5. Of course it won't be easy.
6. Oh you should ask permission first.
7. First of all my parents will be there.
8. All right I will do as you ask.
9. Yes the choice is yours.
10. Well they left a few minutes ago.

Exercise 3. Place commas appropriately.

1. Mom have you seen my blouse?
2. Yes it is in your closet Emily.
3. Great I'll look there first.
4. Please put the books Mark over there.
5. Oh that may have been a good answer.
6. Why I have never seen you Elena so well dressed.
7. First of all I am not the person who did it John.
8. I'm glad Mr. Ing that you came.
9. By the way the bus leaves promptly at noon.
10. Sir I do not know the answer.
11. Young lady where is the department store?
12. Please get the telephone Mike.
13. How are you Mrs. Moore?
14. Of course we will go with you.
15. Good grief I forgot to get Mary.

CHAPTER 6 Commas: Series

> Use **commas** to separate words in a series of three or more items.
> - Use *and* before the last word in the series.
> - Do not use a comma after the last word in the series.

EXAMPLES:

Shoes, socks, *and* pants were thrown on the floor.
    —shoes, socks, and pants = a series

The shirts, blouses, *and* coats were hung in the office.
    —shirts, blouses, and coats = a series

The small cup, red bowl, *and* green napkin were on the table.
    —small cup, red bowl, and green napkin = a series

Exercise 1. Find each series. Add commas and **and** as needed.

1. The puppies were cute noisy hungry.
2. We went on our vacation to Utah Nevada Idaho Washington.
3. We drove through mountains deserts prairies.
4. Juan Anita Mary William stayed after school.
5. They arrived tired dirty exhausted.
6. Gold blue red green are favorite colors of John Kim Ray Beth.
7. The house was old unpainted filthy.
8. The pigs cows chickens ducks were put in the barn by Alice and Jane.
9. Paper crayons scissors are in the closet.
10. Tuesday was cold dark rainy.
11. A car a boat a dog were outside.
12. She lost a comb a bag of pennies a watch.
13. Add ten one four six!
14. We have visited Seattle San Francisco Los Angeles.
15. Emily, pick up the tape the book your coat.

Exercise 2. Write a sentence to include each series. Use commas and **and** as needed.

1. wet, cold, heavy
2. a car, a train, a boat
3. run, jump, throw
4. apples, grapes, lemons
5. head, shoulders, knees, toes

CHAPTER **7** Commas: Compound Sentences

> Use a **comma** before conjunctions like *and*, *or*, and *but* in a compound sentence.

A compound sentence expresses two complete ideas.

EXAMPLES: Texas is a big state. It has many people.
        —2 sentences, 2 complete ideas
Texas is a big state, **and** it has many people.
        —1 sentence, 2 complete Ideas

Joel can go to the store. He can stay home.
Joel can go to the store, **or** he can stay home.

She went to the store. It was closed.
She went to the store, **but** it was closed.

Exercise 1. Combine the following sentences using a comma and the word in parentheses.

1. Many people live here. They work in town. (and)

2. The houses are old. They are built well. (but)

3. Some people have lawns. Some people have gardens. (and)

4. Should our neighbor plant cabbage? Should our neighbor build a fence? (or)

5. You can ride the horse. I will watch. (and)

6. Our house borders a road. It also borders a pasture. (but)

7. You can go to the store by the road. You can go through the pasture. (or)

8. The road is quicker. The pasture has more things to see. (but)

9. Will you go home? Will you stay here? (or)

10. He took the path. She walked down the road. (and)

Exercise 2. What two complete sentences make up each compound sentence? Remove the comma and conjunction. Capitalize the first word for both sentences.

1. The dog slept, and the cat played.

2. Maria went home, and she went to sleep.

3. He dressed himself, and he ate breakfast.

4. The light turned green, but the cars did not move.

5. He is coming now, or he will be left behind.

Exercise 3. All sentences are compound sentences. Underline the conjunction and add a comma where it belongs.

1. Eastern Oregon has high deserts but Western Oregon has lush forests.

2. Lumber is shipped east and cattle are shipped west.

3. People live in large cities or they live in small towns.

4. Some farmers grow vegetables and other farmers grow grass seed.

5. It was raining yesterday but the sun is shining today.

6. Deliveries are made by noon or they aren't made at all.

7. He held the pole and she attached the sign.

8. Juan can ride next or you can return it to me.

9. Both boys rode and I walked.

10. Ten people voted but most people went home.

Exercise 4. Add commas in compound sentences. Not all sentences are compound.

1. My brother and I listened to jazz and rock music.

2. This one is good but that one is better.

3. Half went one way and half went the other way.

4. Are you coming or not?

5. I like it but it's not my favorite.

6. You can come with us or you can stay here.

7. Many berries are small but tasty.

8. Thursday was stormy but Friday was clear.

9. They have cats and dogs but we have horses.

10. I don't enjoy hockey or football.

11. Scott climbed the stairs but Nancy took the elevator.

12. You should study first or you should not take the test.

13. He ran home and opened the closet door.

14. The whistle blew and the parade began.

15. Bring me the cans and bottles.

CHAPTER 8 Commas: Quotation Marks

> **Quotation marks** are used to show the exact words a person speaks.
>
> A **comma** is used to separate the speaker from what is said.

EXAMPLES:
Jane said, " Come in and sit down."
"Come this way," said Jane, "and sit near the door."
"Put those boxes over there," she said.

Be sure to place the comma inside the quotation marks when the speaker follows the quotation.

Exercise 1. Rewrite each sentence and correctly place any needed commas.

1. "Put it over there" said John quickly.

2. She asked "What time did you leave?"

3. Levi warned "Be sure you know how to do it."

4. The class shouted "Oh, that's fantastic!"

5. "It's closer than you think" answered Joan.

6. "If you are confused, ask me" instructed Mrs. Myers.

7. Together they shouted "Look out!"

8. He put it down and said "These are large boxes."

9. Jules replied "They are heavy, too."

10. "There are a dozen more" answered Bill.

11. "Yes" she replied "I would like to go."

12. "Climb over the wall" he called "and come here."

13. "We must walk three more miles" she said.

14. "I was speaking" Gail whispered "to you and to the others."

15. "You must be thirsty" stated Alex.

Exercise 2. Rewrite each as a direct quotation. Add a speaker to each sentence. Add commas and quotation marks properly.

1. Count to ten.

2. Who will answer the phone?

3. Let's go on the train.

4. I have my own opinion.

5. Ask her!

CHAPTER 9 Commas: Appositives

> **Appositives** are words or phrases that rename or identify the words or phrases they follow. Appositives are set off with **commas**.

EXAMPLES: Alex, **my brother**, is home from school.
　　　　　　　—*my brother* renames Alex.
　　　　　　Our neighbors, **the Millers**, are across the street.
　　　　　　　—*the Millers* identifies the neighbors.
　　　　　　They will feed Molly, **our cat**.
　　　　　　　—*our cat* identifies Molly.

Exercise 1. In each sentence below, add commas to set off appositives.

1. Can you call Joan the owner of this car?

2. Walter Glick the actor made few movies.

3. Sally my friend will come with me today.

4. We visited Salem the state capitol.

5. The two workers Alice and Miles finished the job.

6. Jack and Al our cousins will be here soon.

7. How old is Barko your dog?

8. The Queen Mary an oceanliner is docked in California.

9. Our dentist Felicia Roberts is open on Saturday.

10. How far is it to Portland the closest town?

Exercise 2. Add commas as necessary. Not all sentences need commas.

1. Will you ride in the car with us?

2. The two girls Robin and Carol decided to go.

3. Dr. Jefferson an eye doctor can give you an eye examination.

4. The store is closed on the Fourth of July a national holiday.

5. Mrs. Smith a farmer and Mr. James a tailor met for lunch.

6. The friends met near the park for lunch.

7. Ellen my best friend is now living in Virginia.

8. The Fourth of July Independence Day is an annual holiday.

9. Paul the boy next to you is my neighbor.

10. The first car a red Ford is driven by Mrs. Green the mayor.

CHAPTER 10 Apostrophes: Contractions

> A **contraction** is one word made out of two words. An **apostrophe** is used to show where a letter or letters have been left out.

EXAMPLES:
it + is = it's
we + will = we'll
you + are = you're

Exercise I. Fill in the chart.

Two Words	Contraction	Two Words	Contraction
1. it is	_____	21. will not	_____
2. are not	_____	22. should not	_____
3. I am	_____	23. we are	_____
4. _____	she's	24. he is	_____
5. you are	_____	25. could have	_____
6. _____	we'll	26. we have	_____
7. he is	_____	27. they had	_____
8. they are	_____	28. would not	_____
9. _____	I've	29. I had	_____
10. do not	_____	30. she had	_____
11. _____	shouldn't	31. _____	they're
12. _____	won't	32. _____	isn't
13. she had	_____	33. _____	you'll
14. it will	_____	34. _____	hasn't
15. _____	you'd	35. _____	I'll
16. _____	didn't	36. _____	we've
17. were not	_____	37. _____	should've
18. they will	_____	38. _____	they've
19. _____	there's	39. _____	you're
20. there is	_____	40. _____	couldn't

CHAPTER 11 Apostrophes: Possessive Nouns

> **Apostrophes** are used to show possession. Apostrophes are used with singular and plural nouns to show possession.

Remember: A noun names a person, place, or thing.

Use an apostrophe and s ('s) to form the possessive of a singular noun. For one syllable words ending in s, add an apostrophe and s ('s).

Singular Noun		Singular Possessive Form
cat	cat + **'s**	the cat**'s** tail
James	James + **'s**	James**'s** house
woman	woman + **'s**	the woman**'s** home
girl	girl + **'s**	a girl**'s** coat

Use an apostrophe to form the possessive of a singular noun having two or more syllables and ending with the s or z sound.

Singular Noun
2 or more syllables, with s or z sound.   Singular Possessive Form

Collins	Collins + '	Ms. Collins' coat
Perez	Perez + '	Mr. Perez' home
Moses	Moses + '	Moses' brother
Cortez	Cortez + '	Cortez' army

Use an apostrophe to form the possessive of a plural noun ending in s.

Plural Noun		Plural Possessive Form
girls	girls + '	the girls' reports
Joneses	Joneses + '	the Joneses' home
wolves	wolves + '	the wolves' dens
stories	stories + '	the stories' endings

Use an apostrophe and s ('s) to form the possessive form of plural nouns not ending in s.

Plural Noun		Possessive Form
children	children + **'s**	the children**'s** school
women	women + **'s**	the women**'s** meeting
salesmen	salemen + **'s**	the salesmen**'s** work
people	people + **'s**	the people**'s** support

Exercise 1. Write the possessive form for each word. Use an apostrophe and s (**'s**) or an apostrophe (**'**) alone.

1. man	6. boys	11. baby
2. women	7. Mr. Gomez	12. babies
3. Charles	8. actor	13. country
4. schools	9. child	14. countries
5. dollars	10. children	15. horses

Exercise 2. Rewrite each phrase forming the correct possessive form for each underlined noun.

1. Martin Luther <u>King</u> birthday	11. his <u>father</u> hat
2. two <u>girls</u> shoes	12. a <u>lady</u> purse
3. A <u>cat</u> paw	13. the <u>babies</u> strollers
4. New <u>Year</u> Day	14. the <u>bird</u> nest
5. a <u>sheep</u> wool	15. a <u>deer</u> horn
6. one <u>child</u> games	16. <u>Maria</u> house
7. two <u>children</u> games	17. <u>mice</u> hole
8. one <u>student</u> grades	18. the <u>family</u> home
9. Mr. <u>Fairbanks</u> cat	19. many <u>spiders</u> webs
10. <u>James</u> book	20. Mr. <u>Fuentes</u> home

Exercise 3. Find the noun showing possession. Write its correct possessive form.

1. Was the light bulb Thomas Edison invention?

2. Which way to the men and women dressing rooms?

3. That is the Schultz house.

4. Emily, Jane, and Marta bicycles are in the driveway.

5. Our neighbor father sells children shoes.

6. All of the animals meals were brought by the keeper.

7. Marie Torres mother brought her coat.

8. Everyone attention was focused on the magician hand.

9. Is this pencil James?

10. Please bring all of the boys shoes here.

CHAPTER 12 Quotation Marks

> **Quotation marks** are used by writers to show a speaker's exact words.
>
> Direct quotations begin with a capital letter.

EXAMPLES:
"**H**ow far is it to school?" asked Doug.
Sara answered, "**I**t is two miles."
"**D**id you read the sign?" said Doug.

Place periods, question marks, and exclamation marks within direct quotation marks. Place commas inside quotation marks only when the speaker follows the quotation.

EXAMPLES:
He yelled, "**S**top that!"
She asked, "**I**s that yours?"
"**H**ow far," asked Emily, "is it to the store?"

Exercise 1. Place quotation marks correctly.

1. Have you been here before? asked Jane.

2. Yes, about two years ago, replied Stan with a smile.

3. Do you both know when the show starts? asked Mrs. Kozol.

4. Jane thought and said, At 8:30, as I remember.

5. That's right, answered Mrs. Kozol.

6. And it should end, explained Stan, at about 10:00 P.M.

7. Come this way, said the usher.

8. They stopped at row 5, and Jane said, Here are our seats.

9. We are here in plenty of time, whispered Mrs. Kozol.

10. I am looking forward, said Stan, to this show.

Exercise 2. Place quotation marks correctly.

1. What is the question? asked James.

2. Kim replied, Did you enjoy the book?

3. Yes, answered James, it was very enjoyable.

4. I liked the book, too, interrupted Meryl.

5. It's a favorite among kids in our class, continued James.

6. Stop that! yelled Mr. Peters.

7. Why? asked his daughter, Julie.

8. Because you might hurt your arms, answered Mr. Peters.

9. Not wanting to argue with her father, Julie said, Can I practice tomorrow?

10. You can practice tomorrow, agreed Mr. Peters.

Exercise 3. Rewrite each sentence as a direct quotation. Use the person indicated in parentheses as the speaker. Put the speaker at the (1) beginning, (2) in the middle, or (3) at the end of the quotation.

1. It's fourteen miles to the next town. (3 Steven)

2. We can drive miles and miles without seeing anyone. (1 Karen)

3. I wonder how far kids travel to school each day? (2 Steven)

4. I don't know, but it is a long distance. (1 Earl)

5. This is different from what we are used to. (2 Karen)

Capitalization and Punctuation

Review 2: Punctuation

Read the following passages. Place all necessary commas and quotation marks. Add apostrophes to contractions, and apostrophes and s ('s) for possessive nouns.

Review 1.

Mr. Jones I want this letter to go to Mr. J.R. Phillips president of United Shoes dictated Mrs. Ethel Moore. The address is 1427 North First Street Canton Ohio.

Mrs. Moore dictated this letter and she dictated two other letters. Mrs. Moore two other letters were sent to Ames Iowa and Ottawa Ontario Canada.

Review 2.

They brought sandwiches sodas and dessert_ Bill said   Well I think we should eat over there.

Yes said Carole that will be fine.

They walked across the field down the hill and sat near the lake. Bill the older brother took a letter from his pocket.

Tomorrow is Dad birthday he reminded Carole.

Did you get his present with John Maria and James money? asked Carole.

Yes Well all give it to him tomorrow but we cant do it until the afternoon said Bill.

Review 3.

• All twelve students coats were in a pile. Elena was on top and she found it quickly.

• A lady purse a man hat and a pair of gloves were left. They were gathered by Mr. Norton the janitor. He placed them in a box and he sent the box to the office.

• All cities problems cant be solved overnight. No they must be solved slowly and they must be solved correctly.

Capitalization and Punctuation

Final Assessment Test

A. Capitalization, Abbreviation, and Ending Marks. Rewrite each sentence. Use capital letters. Punctuate abbreviations. End sentences with the correct ending mark (. , ? , !).

1. can you remember where mr lopez works

2. he shouted madly, "don't do that"

3. on tuesday, may 3rd, i will move to europe

4. their father said, "do you know why i want to go"

5. my brother and i were born in denver, colorado

6. how close does dr cowns live to the pacific ocean

7. she said, "our address is on elm street near crescent rd"

8. here is how i abbreviate those days of the week: mon , tues , wed, and thurs

9. william m moore lives at 127 park av, oakland, california

10. on what day does christmas fall this year

B. Commas. Rewrite each sentence. Place commas correctly.

1. Mr. Stein did you call me on Tuesday November 23rd?

2. Walter Glick the actor said to the crowd "See what I mean?"

3. This is a good one but that one is better.

4. The paper crayons and paint are in the cabinet Mrs. Jones.

5. John Anita and Mary stayed here and the others left last night.

6. Driver take me to 1257 Hillview Lane Eugene Oregon.

7. The oceanliner the Queen Mary is docked at Long Beach California.

8. They arrived tired dirty and exhausted on Wednesday May 23 1990.

9. The captain shouted "Call two cars three trucks and one van."

10. Of course Christmas December 25 1960 was over thirty years ago.

11. Merle our cousin has three but Tom has more.

12. Send an answer to 10 Blaine Av. Winnipig Manitoba before Monday.

Final Assessment Test

C. Contractions. Form a contraction from each pair of words.

1. they will _____

2. have not _____

3. I would _____

4. he is _____

5. they have _____

6. she had _____

7. could have _____

8. should not _____

9. you will _____

10. you are _____

11. I am _____

12. is not _____

D. Possessives. Rewrite each phrase, forming the correct possessive.

1. Mr. Gomez house

_____

2. the cat tail

_____

3. the people choice

_____

4. the babies strollers

_____

5. six students work

_____

6. Max Diner

_____

7. two ladies purses

_____

8. ten sheep wool

_____

9. Mrs. James car

_____

10. womens store

_____

11. the bees hive

_____

12. the spider web

_____

Capitalization and Punctuation

GARLIC PRESS

Answers
Beginning Assessment Test
pages 7–8

A. Capitalization. Abbreviation, and Ending Marks. Rewrite each sentence. Use capital letters. Punctuate abbreviations. Use the correct ending marks.

1. **W**ill you come with me to the **F**ounder's **D**ay **P**arade**?**

2. **H**e and **I** will meet you there**.**

3. **T**he boy asked **E**mily and **E**lena for a ride**.**

4. **D**on't do that**!**

5. **D**oes **Dr. L**inda **L. S**mith live here**?**

6. We went to **F**lorida in **J**une to see **D**isney **W**orld**.**

7. Our leader said, "**S**top! "

8. The first **A**merican **P**resident was **G**eorge **W**ashington**.**

9. Next **T**uesday at 3:00 **P. M. ,** we will arrive in **C**anada**.**

10. He said, "**T**omorrow is **V**alentine's **D**ay**.** "

11. I am not sure if **I** called **M**rs. **D. C. A**lexis**.**

12. Did you include our trip to **O**regon and **C**rater **L**ake**?**

B. Commas. Rewrite each sentence. Place commas correctly.

1. Today is Wednesday**,** July 6**,** 1990.

2. I went to the store**,** and she went home.

3. Mr. Moore**,** our teacher**,** called my parents last night.

4. Yes**,** we will fly to Oakland**,** California.

5. John spoke quietly**,** "They left their hats**,** coats**,** and towels here."

6. Please take care of our dogs**,** cats**,** and parrot.

7. Thank you**,** Marie**,** for your map of Denver**,** Colorado.

8. I like it**,** but it is not my favorite.

9. "It's closer than you think**,**" remarked Juan.

10. By the way**,** the letter was mailed May 3**,** 1946**,** by my uncle.

11. Gold**,** red**,** green**,** and blue are the favorite colors of Jane**,** Alice**,** and Bill.

12. Only four people**,** Jill**,** can go with Becky.

13. How old is Barko**,** your dog?

14. Together they shouted**,** "Look out!"

15. He held the pole**,** and she attached the sign.

C. Apostrophes. Form a contraction for each pair of words.

1. I would–**I'd**

2. you are–**you're**

3. do not–**don't**

4. they had–**they'd**

5. they have–**they've**

6. could not–**couldn't**

7. she had–**she'd**

8. we have–**we've**

9. I will–**I'll**

10. he is–**he's**

11. could have–**could've**

12. should not–**shouldn't**

D. Possessives. Rewrite each phrase forming the correct possessive.

1. Mary name–Mary**'s** name

2. one child game–one child**'s** game

3. four children game–four children**'s** game

4. the Jones yard–the Jones**'s** yard

5. several stores signs–several stores' signs

6. many dogs collars–many dogs' collars

7. Ms. Lopez house–Ms. Lopez' house

8. both nurses smiles–both nurses' smiles

9. J.B. Doris car–J.B. Doris' car

10. the spider web–the spider**'s** web

11. two days work–two days' work

12. New Year Day–New Year**'s** Day

Answers

I and First Words, Exercise 1. Page 9.

1. **T**he morning was clear and brisk.
2. **T**hey awoke before their parents did.
3. "**I**'m glad we came on this camping trip," said Elena.
4. **H**er brother replied, "**I**t has been more than **I** expected."
5. "**A**re you two awake?" came their father's voice.
6. **E**ric answered, "**W**e just woke up."
7. **A**fter breakfast, the family decided to go for a hike.
8. "**T**he trail begins over here, **I** think," said his father.
9. **T**hey walked to the trailhead.
10. **P**ointing to the sign, Elena said, "**I** think we should take this trail."
11. **T**hey all agreed.
12. "**W**e can have lunch at the lake," said her father.
13. "**Y**es, but **I** also want to go for a swim," added Eric.
14. **T**heir father said, "**B**efore we go, be sure to take your lunch and swimsuit."
15. **B**oth children answered together, "**W**e will."

Proper Nouns, Exercise 1. Page 10.

1. On our visit to the state capitol, we met **G**overnor **E**vans.
2. Sue and **J**ames are brother and sister.
3. The sign read, "**M**rs. **F**elicia **R**. **J**erome, **M.D.**"
4. We met **S**enator **G**arcia, too.
5. One neighbor is **T. B. G**oodyear, and the other is **C**aptain **M**ary **L**utz.
6. Have you seen **A**lbert **L. R**iveria, **S**r., or **M**r. and **M**rs. **T**horn?
7. Who is the president of the club?
8. **A**mbassador **W**arren introduced us to the other ambassadors.
9. The lottery was won by **J. M**ichael **C**hang and his sister, **J**ane.
10. The principal of our school is **M**rs. **V**irginia **D**aniels.
11. The first prize was presented to my **U**ncle **L**eon.
12. My sister and grandmother went shopping.
13. My friend **M**arsha has a puppy that she named **M**iles.
14. The order is for **J**ohn, **M**arie, **T**erry, **G**ail and **M**ax.
15. Their aunt and uncle finally met **M**iss **G**reen.

Particular Places, Exercise 2. Page 11.

1. The **A**ndes **M**ountains are in **C**hile and **A**rgentina.
2. Which is larger, **L**os **A**ngeles, **C**alifornia, or **D**enver, **C**olorado?
3. Lake **P**lacid is in **N**ew **Y**ork.
4. The **M**ississippi **R**iver flows from **M**innesota to the **G**ulf of **M**exico.
5. The store is at the corner of **P**ark **L**ane and **C**oburg **R**oad.
6. You might need a reservation to stay in **Y**osemite **N**ational **P**ark.
7. The smallest state is **R**hode **I**sland.
8. Drive home by way of **O**ak **G**rove, **G**olden **V**alley, and **M**urphy.
9. Canada, the **U**nited **S**tates, and **M**exico are part of **N**orth **A**merica.
10. The **L**ewis and **C**lark **E**xpedition reached the **P**acific **O**cean in 1803.
11. We went backpacking in the **R**ocky **M**ountains.
12. The **H**awaiian **I**slands are not in the **A**tlantic **O**cean.
13. The **G**reen **M**ountains are in **V**ermont.
14. Deliver this to 246 **W**est **A**ndover **S**treet.
15. Alberta, **B**ritish **C**olumbia, and **M**anitoba are provinces in **C**anada.

Particular Things, Exercise 3. Pages 11–12.

1. We are to meet you on **W**ednesday, **M**arch 3, in **O**maha, **N**ebraska.
2. This year, **C**hristmas falls on **S**unday.
3. The **I**rish like to celebrate **S**t. **P**atrick's **D**ay.
4. How many months are between **M**ay and **D**ecember?
5. The card shop is open on **T**hursday.
6. The **W**orld **C**ar **A**ssociation holds its yearly meeting in **A**pril.
7. Let's stop and get a **B**ig **M**ac.
8. I already know what I will be for **H**alloween.
9. The **P**ortland **C**hamber of **C**ommerce has a parade every **L**abor **D**ay.
10. The **B**ank of **M**ontreal is open until 5:00 P.M. **M**onday through **F**riday.
11. The **A**merican **L**ung **A**ssociation has a special event each year.
12. The **F**rench settled here before the turn of the century.
13. John's father works for **L**ane **C**ounty **H**ealth **D**epartment.
14. Buy a quart of **C**arnation's **M**ilk and a case of **C**oca-**C**ola.
15. How many cards do you need for **V**alentine's **D**ay?
16. The **A**merican **C**ivil **W**ar was fought between 1861 and 1865.
17. The **N**ative **A**merican dancers will perform during the **F**estival of **L**ights.
18. My membership in the **S**ierra **C**lub expires in **D**ecember.
19. That club meets every other week.
20. Did you donate blood to the **R**ed **C**ross?

Capitalization, Exercise 4. Page 12.

Have I told you about **M**ilton **J**ohnston? He is my uncle. We visit him every year at **E**aster. We drive to **K**alispell, **M**ontana, to see him. He lives on the south end of **M**ain **S**treet, across the street from the **R**ocky **M**ountain **M**useum.

Sometimes we go to **F**lathead **L**ake and fish. And sometimes we visit **G**lacier **N**ational **P**ark or **W**aterton **G**lacier **I**nternational **P**eace **P**ark. The **W**aterton **G**lacier **I**nternational **P**eace **P**ark crosses the **U**nited **S**tates and **C**anada border and extends into the province of **A**lberta.

When we go to either park, we cross the **C**ontinental **D**ivide. We have visited the town of **S**t. **M**ary. We have also visited the nearby **B**lackfoot **I**ndian **R**eservation.

My **U**ncle **M**ilton tells us stories. He tells us about working for the **G**reat **N**orthern **R**ailroad. And he tells us about meeting famous people. He once met **C**harles **R**ussell, the painter.

Ending Marks and Sentences, Exercise 1. Page 14.

1. Can you remember the color? **Inter.**
2. Put the books on the shelf. **Imper.**
3. Look at that accident! **Excl.** or **Imper.**
4. The bus left them behind. **Decl.**
5. Please don't forget to lock the door. **Imper.**
6. Did you lock the door? **Inter.**
7. What a fine new car! **Excl.** or **Decl.**
8. The sun is setting over the hills. **Decl.**

Answers

9. Would you take this to my home? **Inter.**
10. The next town is only a few miles away. **Decl.**

Ending Marks and Sentences, Exercise 2. Page 14.

The morning was cold. Dr. Ann Moore and her husband, J. B. Moore, drove along. Would it snow**?** They wondered. It was 9:30 A. M. when they arrived at the cabin.

J. B. got out of the car. Did he have a key to the cabin**?** Was 110 Center St. the correct address**?** He asked Ann. It was.

"What a beautiful cabin!" exclaimed Ann. The long drive from Albany, Calif., had been worth it. They would stay until Wed. morning.

Capitalization & Punctuation Review. Page 15.

I have a friend. **H**is name is **C**harles **S**moot, but I call him **C**huck.

Chuck lives in the **W**illamette **V**alley of **O**regon. **H**ave you ever heard of **E**ugene, **O**regon? **E**ugene is his hometown.

Chuck goes to Washington **S**chool. **H**e plays many **s**chool sports and belongs to several **s**chool **c**lubs.

Chuck and I met through the mail. **H**is teacher and mine started a writing exchange between students. Chuck wrote to me first, and then I answered. Or was it the other way around**?**

Chuck has told me that he has a **s**ister named **E**llen. His mother, who works at the **U**niversity of **O**regon, is a **u**niversity teacher. His father is **p**resident of a small business called **L**ane **C**ounty **L**umber.

Chuck does many things with his family in the **w**inter. **T**hey can downhill ski at **M**t. **B**achelor, or they can cross country ski anywhere near the **T**hree Sisters **W**ilderness **A**rea.

The nearby **C**ascade **M**ountains are beautiful. **T**he **S**moots can hike or camp in the summer. **T**hey don't have to travel far.

This summer, I will travel across **C**anada and the **U**nited **S**tates to stay with the **S**moots. I will travel either by **G**reyhound **B**us or **U**nited **A**irlines. I will be there in **A**ugust. Doesn't that sound exciting**?**

Dates and Addresses, Exercise 1. Page 16.

1. Tuesday, June 29
2. September 1, 1928
3. Montreal, Quebec
4. Sunday, April 24, 1988
5. New York City, New York
6. March 14, 1945
7. Paris, France
8. Seattle, Washington
9. Mexico City, Mexico
10. Friday, July 9
11. San Francisco, California
12. Saturday, August 23
13. London, England
14. October 13, 1985
15. Wednesday, May 19, 1988
16. Atlanta, Georgia
17. September 11, 1960
18. St. Louis, Missouri
19. Saturday, November 22
20. March 24, 1782

Dates and Addresses, Exercise 2. Page 17.

1. Today's date is January 11, 1988.
2. The last day of the year is Tuesday, December 31.
3. Why is July 4, 1776, such an important date?
4. Address the letter to 23 First Av., Portland, Oregon.
5. How far is it from Rome, Italy, to Moscow, Russia?
6. On Tuesday, September 10, 1976, she will be fourteen.
7. The business was founded June 1, 1924, in Ottawa, Ontario.
8. He was born in Newton, Vermont, but moved to San Diego, California,
9. Toronto, Ontario, is not far from Buffalo, New York.
10. The office on 1246 Hillview is open until Friday, August 2.

Dates and Addresses, Exercise 3. Page 17.

1. 45 Taft St.
   Minneapolis, Minnesota 55413
   December 31, 1948
2. 999 South Jason St.
   Saint John, New Brunswick E2K 2A9
   November 22, 1911
3. 62 North 47th Av.
   Glendale, Arizona 85301
   October 31, 1977
4. 8593 College Av.
   Ft. Meyers, Florida 33919
   January 11, 1997
5. 6561 Beach St.
   Buena Park, California 90621
   February 30, 2007
6. 460 Horner Av.
   Toronto, Ontario M8W 4X2
   March 12, 2008

Dates and Addresses, Exercise 4. Page 17.

1. They arrived here in March 1989.
2. Send this letter to Mexico City, Mexico, before next week.
3. The letter was sent May 12, 1990, and arrived three days later.
4. You can drive from Toronto, Ontario, to Montreal, Quebec, in one day.
5. The event took place in September of 1912.
6. Deliver this to 127 Maple St., Springfield, Oregon, by tomorrow,
7. Los Angeles, California, is nearly an eight hour drive from Phoenix, Arizona.
8. January 11, 1946, is my birth date.
9. He flew from Ontario, Canada, to Seattle, Washington.
10. The letter was postmarked Panama City, Panama, on November 22, 1911.

Introductory Words/Nouns of Address, Exercise 1. Page 18.

1. Did you call me, Mr. Stein?
2. Lee, make sure the door is shut.
3. Please, Sara, watch what you are doing.
4. Give this to John, Bill.
5. Robert, what is the date tomorrow?

Answers

6. Thank you, Susan, for remembering to get the cake.
7. Scott, please help Syd with the dinner.
8. Mr. and Mrs. Rovetta, here is your table.
9. I believe, sir, you are wrong.
10. We are going home first, Emily.

Introductory Words/Nouns of Address, Exercise 2. Page 19.

1. Yes, you have been successful!
2. By the way, how far is it?
3. Well, my brother will help me.
4. No, you must first complete the assignment.
5. Of course, it won't be easy.
6. Oh, you should ask permission first.
7. First of all, my parents will be there.
8. All right, I will do as you ask.
9. Yes, the choice is yours.
10. Well, they left a few minutes ago.

Introductory Words/Nouns of Address, Exercise 3. Page 19.

1. Mom, have you seen my blouse?
2. Yes, it is in your closet, Emily.
3. Great, I'll look there first.
4. Please put the books, Mark, over there.
5. Oh, that may have been a good answer.
6. Why, I have never seen you, Elena, so well dressed.
7. First of all, I am not the person who did it, John.
8. I'm glad, Mr. Ing, that you came.
9. By the way, the bus leaves promptly at noon.
10. Sir, I do not know the answer.
11. Young lady, where is the department store?
12. Please get the telephone, Mike.
13. How are you, Mrs. Moore?
14. Of course, we will go with you.
15. Good grief, I forgot to get Mary.

Commas in Series, Exercise 1. Page 20.

1. The puppies were cute, noisy, **and** hungry.
2. We went on our vacation to Utah, Nevada, Idaho, **and** Washington.
3. We drove through mountains, deserts, **and** prairies.
4. Juan, Anita, Mary, **and** William stayed after school.
5. They arrived tired, dirty, **and** exhausted.
6. Gold, blue, red, **and** green are favorite colors of John, Kim, Ray, **and** Beth.
7. The house was old, unpainted, **and** filthy.
8. The pigs, cows, chickens, **and** ducks were put in the barn by Alice and Jane.
9. Paper, crayons, **and** scissors are in the closet.
10. Tuesday was cold, dark, **and** rainy.
11. A car, a boat, **and** a dog were outside.
12. She lost a comb, a bag of pennies, **and** a watch.
13. Add ten, one, four, **and** six!
14. We have visited Seattle, San Francisco, **and** Los Angeles.
15. Emily, pick up the tape, the book, **and** your coat.

Commas in Series, Exercise 2. Page 20.

Answers will vary.

Commas in Compound Sentences, Exercise 1. Page 21.

1. Many people live here, **and** they work in town.
2. The houses are old, **but** they are built well.
3. Some people have lawns, **and** some people have gardens.
4. Should our neighbor plant cabbage, **or** should our neighbor build a fence?
5. You can ride the horse, **and** I will watch.
6. Our house borders a road, **but** it also borders a pasture.
7. You can go to the store by the road, **or** you can go through the pasture.
8. The road is quicker, **but** the pasture has more things to see.
9. Will you go home, **or** will you stay here?
10. He took the path, **and** she walked down the road.

Commas in Compound Sentences, Exercise 2. Page 21.

1. The dog slept. The cat played.
2. Maria went home. She went to sleep.
3. He dressed himself. He ate breakfast.
4. The light turned green. The cars did not move.
5. He is coming now. He will be left behind.

Commas in Compound Sentences, Exercise 3. Page 22.

1. Eastern Oregon has high deserts, <u>but</u> Western Oregon has lush forests.
2. Lumber is shipped east, <u>and</u> cattle are shipped west.
3. People live in large cities, <u>or</u> they live in small towns.
4. Some farmers grow vegetables, <u>and</u> other farmers grow grass seed.
5. It was raining yesterday, <u>but</u> the sun is shining today.
6. Deliveries are made by noon, <u>or</u> they aren't made at all.
7. He held the pole, <u>and</u> she attached the sign.
8. Juan can ride next, <u>or</u> you can return it to me.
9. Both boys rode, <u>and</u> I walked.
10. Ten people voted, <u>but</u> most people went home.

Commas in Compound Sentences, Exercise 4. Page 22.

1. My brother and I listened to jazz and rock music.
2. This one is good, but that one is better.
3. Half went one way, and half went the other way.
4. Are you coming or not?
5. I like it, but it's not my favorite.
6. You can come with us, or you can stay here.
7. Many berries are small but tasty.
8. Thursday was stormy, but Friday was clear.
9. They have cats and dogs, but we have horses.
10. I don't enjoy hockey or football.
11. Scott climbed the stairs, but Nancy took the elevator.
12. You should study first, or you should not take the test.
13. He ran home and opened the closet door.
14. The whistle blew, and the parade began.
15. Bring me the cans and bottles.

Answers

Commas and Quotation Marks, Exercise 1. Page 23.

1. "Put it over there," said John quickly.
2. She asked, "What time did you leave?"
3. Levi warned, "Be sure you know how to do it."
4. The class shouted, "Oh, that's fantastic!"
5. "It's closer than you think," answered Joan.
6. "If you are confused, ask me," instructed Mrs. Myers.
7. Together they shouted, "Look out!"
8. He put it down and said, "These are large boxes."
9. Jules replied, "They are heavy, too."
10. "There are a dozen more," answered Bill.
11. "Yes," she replied, "I would like to go."
12. "Climb over the wall," he called, "and come here."
13. "We must walk three more miles," she said.
14. "I was speaking," Gail whispered, "to you and to the others."
15. "You must be thirsty," stated Alex.

Commas and Quotation Marks, Exercise 2. Page 23.

Answers will vary.

Commas and Appositives, Exercise 1. Page 24.

1. Can you call Joan, the owner of this car?
2. Walter Glick, the actor, made few movies.
3. Sally, my friend, will come with me today.
4. We visited Salem, the state capitol.
5. The two workers, Alice and Miles, finished the job.
6. Jack and Al, our cousins, will be here soon.
7. How old is Barko, your dog?
8. The Queen Mary, an oceanliner, is docked in California.
9. Our dentist, Felicia Roberts, is open on Saturday.
10. How far is it to Portland, the closest town?

Commas and Appositives, Exercise 2. Page 24.

1. Will you ride in the car with us?
2. The two girls, Robin and Carol, decided to go.
3. Dr. Jefferson, an eye doctor, can give you an eye examination.
4. The store is closed on the Fourth of July, a national holiday.
5. Mrs. Smith, a farmer, and Mr. James, a tailor, met for lunch.
6. The friends met near the park for lunch.
7. Ellen, my best friend, is now living in Virginia.
8. The Fourth of July, Independence Day, is an annual holiday.
9. Paul, the boy next to you, is my neighbor.
10. The first car, a red Ford, is driven by Mrs. Green, the mayor.

Apostrophes and Contractions, Exercise 1. Page 25.

	Two Words	Contraction		Two Words	Contraction
1.	it is	**it's**	21.	will not	**won't**
2.	are not	**aren't**	22.	should not	**shouldn't**
3.	I am	**I'm**	23.	we are	**we're**
4.	**she is**	she's	24.	he is	**he's**
5.	you are	**you're**	25.	could have	**could've**
6.	**we will**	we'll	26.	we have	**we've**
7.	he is	**he's**	27.	they had	**they'd**
8.	they are	**they're**	28.	would not	**wouldn't**
9.	**I have**	I've	29.	I had	**I'd**
10.	do not	**don't**	30.	she had	**she'd**
11.	**should not**	shouldn't	31.	**they are**	they're
12.	**will not**	won't	32.	**is not**	isn't
13.	she had	**she'd**	33.	**you will**	you'll
14.	it will	**it'll**	34.	**has not**	hasn't
15.	**you had**	you'd	35.	**I will**	I'll
16.	**did not**	didn't	36.	**we have**	we've
17.	were not	**weren't**	37.	**should have**	should've
18.	they will	**they'll**	38.	**they have**	they've
19.	**there is**	there's	39.	**you are**	you're
20.	there is	**there's**	40.	**could not**	couldn't

Apostrophes and Possessive Nouns, Exercise 1. Page 27.

1. man**'s**	6. boys**'**	11. baby**'s**
2. women**'s**	7. Mr. Gomez**'**	12. babies**'**
3. Charles**'s**	8. actor**'s**	13. country**'s**
4. schools**'**	9. child**'s**	14. countries**'**
5. dollars**'**	10. children**'s**	15. horses**'**

Apostrophes and Possessive Nouns. Exercise 2. Page 27.

1. M. L. King**'s** birthday
2. two girls**'** shoes
3. the cat**'s** paw
4. New Year**'s** Day
5. a sheep**'s** wool
6. one child**'s** games
7. two children**'s** games
8. one student**'s** grades
9. Mr. Fairbanks**'** cat
10. James**'s** book
11. his father**'s** hat
12. a lady**'s** purse
13. the babies**'** strollers
14. the bird**'s** nest
15. a deer**'s** horn
16. Maria**'s** house
17. mice**'s** hole
18. the family**'s** home
19. many spiders**'** webs
20. Mr. Fuentes**'** home

Apostrophes and Possessive Nouns, Exercise 3. Page 27.

1. Was the light bulb Thomas Edison**'s** invention?
2. Which way to the men**'s** and women**'s** dressing rooms?
3. That is the Schultz**'s** house.
4. Emily**'s**, Jane**'s**, and Marta**'s** bicycles are in the driveway.
5. Our neighbor**'s** father sells children**'s** shoes.
6. All of the animals**'** meals were brought by the keeper.
7. Marie Torres**'** mother brought her coat.
8. Everyone**'s** attention was focused on the magician**'s** hand.
9. Is this pencil James**'s**?
10. Please bring all of the boys**'** shoes here.

Answers

1. "Have you been here before?" asked Jane.
2. "Yes, about two years ago," replied Stan with a smile.
3. "Do you both know when the show starts?" asked Mrs. Kozol.
4. Jane thought and said, "At 8:30, as I remember."
5. "That's right," answered Mrs. Kozol.
6. "And it should end," explained Stan, "at about 10:00 P.M."
7. "Come this way," said the usher.
8. They stopped at row 5, and Jane said, "Here are our seats."
9. "We are here in plenty of time," whispered Mrs. Kozol.
10. "I am looking forward," said Stan, "to this show."

1. "What is the question?" asked James.
2. Kim replied, "Did you enjoy the book?"
3. "Yes," answered James, "it was very enjoyable."
4. "I liked the book, too," interrupted Meryl.
5. "It's a favorite among kids in our class," continued James.
6. "Stop that!" yelled Mr. Peters.
7. "Why?" asked his daughter, Julie.
8. "Because you might hurt your arms," answered Mr. Peters.
9. Not wanting to argue with her father, Julie said, "Can I practice tomorrow?"
10. "You can practice tomorrow," agreed Mr. Peters.

(Possible answers)

1. "It's fourteen miles to the next town," **said Steven**.
2. **Karen said,** "We can drive miles and miles without seeing anyone."
3. "I wonder how far," **said Steven,** "kids travel to school each day?"
4. **Earl remarked,** "I don't know, but it is a long distance."
5. "This is different," **complained Karen,** "from what we are used to."

Review 1.

"Mr. Jones, I want this letter to go to Mr. J.R. Phillips, president of United Shoes," dictated Mrs. Ethel Moore. "The address is 1427 North First Street, Canton, Ohio."

Mrs. Moore dictated this letter, and she dictated two other letters. Mrs. Moore's two other letters were sent to Ames, Iowa, and Ottawa, Ontario, Canada.

Review 2.

They brought sandwiches, sodas, and dessert. Bill said, "Well, I think we should eat over there."

"Yes," said Carole, "that will be fine."

They walked across the field, down the hill, and sat near the lake. Bill, the older brother, took a letter from his pocket.

"Tomorrow is Dad**'s** birthday," he reminded Carole.

"Did you get his present with John**'s**, Maria**'s**, and James**'s** money?" asked Carole.

"Yes. We'll all give it to him tomorrow, but we can't do it until the afternoon," said Bill.

Review 3.

• All twelve students' coats were in a pile. Elena**'s** was on top, and she found it quickly.

• A lady**'s** purse, a man**'s** hat, and a pair of gloves were left. They were gathered by Mr. Norton, the janitor. He placed them in a box, and he sent the box to the office.

• All cities' problems can't be solved overnight. No, they must be solved slowly, and they must be solved correctly.

Answers
Final Assessment Test
pages 31–32

A. Capitalization, Abbreviation, and Ending Marks. Rewrite each sentence. Use capital letters. Punctuate abbreviations. End sentences with the correct ending mark (. , ? , or !).

1. **C**an you remember where **Mr. L**opez works**?**

2. **H**e shouted madly, "**D**on't do that!"

3. **O**n Tuesday, **M**ay 3rd, **I** will move to **E**urope.

4. **T**heir father said, "**D**o you know why **I** want to go**?**"

5. **M**y brother and **I** were born in **D**enver, **C**olorado.

6. **H**ow close does **Dr. C**owns live to the **P**acific **O**cean**?**

7. **S**he said, "**O**ur address is on **E**lm **S**treet near **C**rescent **R**d."

8. **H**ere is how **I** abbreviate those days of the week: **M**on., **T**ues., **W**ed., and **T**hurs.

9. **W**illiam **M. M**oore lives at 127 **P**ark **A**v., **O**akland, **C**alifornia.

10. **O**n what day does **C**hristmas fall this year**?**

9. The captain shouted, "Call two cars, three trucks, and one van."

10. Of course, Christmas, December 25, 1960, was over thirty years ago.

11. Merle, our cousin, has three, but Tom has more.

12. Send an answer to 10 Blaine Av., Winnipig, Manitoba, before Monday.

C. Contractions. Form a contraction from each pair of words.

1. they will–**they'll**   7. could have–**could've**

2. have not–**haven't**   8. should not–**shouldn't**

3. I would–**I'd**   9. you will–**you'll**

4. he is–**he's**   10. you are–**you're**

5. they have–**they've**   11. I am–**I'm**

6. she had–**she'd**   12. is not–**isn't**

B. Commas. Rewrite each sentence. Place commas correctly.

1. Mr. Stein, did you call me on Tuesday, November 23rd?

2. Walter Glick, the actor, said to the crowd, "See what I mean?"

3. This is a good one, but that one is better.

4. The paper, crayons, and paint are in the cabinet, Mrs. Jones.

5. John, Anita, and Mary stayed here, and the others left last night.

6. Driver, take me to 1257 Hillview Lane, Eugene, Oregon.

7. The oceanliner, the Queen Mary, is docked at Long Beach, California.

8. They arrived tired, dirty, and exhausted on Wednesday, May 23, 1990.

D. Possessives. Rewrite each phrase forming the correct possessive.

1. Mr. Gomez' house   7. two ladies' purses

2. the cat**'s** tail   8. ten sheep**'s** wool

3. the people**'s** choice   9. Mrs. James**'s** car

4. the babies' strollers 10. women**'s** stores

5. six students' work   11. the bees' hive

6. Max**'s** Diner   12. the spider**'s** web

ENGLISH SERIES

The **Straight Forward English** series is designed to measure, teach, review, and master specific English skills. All pages are reproducible and include answers to exercises and tests.

Capitalization & Punctuation
GP-032 • 40 pages
I and First Words; Proper Nouns; Ending Marks and Sentences; Commas; Apostrophes; Quotation Marks.

Nouns & Pronouns
GP-033 • 40 pages
Singular and Plural Nouns; Common and Proper Nouns; Concrete and Abstract Nouns; Collective Nouns; Possessive Pronouns; Pronouns and Contractions; Subject and Object Pronouns.

Verbs
GP-034 • 40 pages
Action Verbs; Linking Verbs; Verb Tense; Subject-Verb Agreement; Spelling Rules for Tense; Helping Verbs; Irregular Verbs; Past Participles.

Sentences
GP-041 • 40 pages
Sentences; Subject and Predicate; Sentence Structures.

Adjectives & Adverbs
GP-035 • 40 pages
Proper Adjectives; Articles; Demonstrative Adjectives; Comparative Adjectives; Special Adjectives: Good and Bad; -ly Adverbs; Comparative Adverbs; Good-Well and Bad-Badly.

Prepositions, Conjunctions and Interjections
GP-043 • 40 pages
Recognizing Prepositions; Object of the Preposition; Prepositional Phrases; Prepositional Phrases as Adjectives and Adverbs; Faulty Reference; Coordinating, Correlative and Subordinate Conjunctions.

ADVANCED ENGLISH SERIES

Get It Right!
GP-148 • 144 pages
Organized into four sections, **Get It Right!** is designed to teach writing skills commonly addressed in the standardized testing in the early grades: Spelling, Mechanics, Usage, and Proofreading. Overall the book includes 100 lessons, plus reviews and skill checks.

All-In-One English
GP-107 • 112 pages
The **All-In-One** is a master book to the Straight Forward English Series.
Under one cover it has included the important English skills of capitalization, punctuation, and all eight parts of speech. Each selection of the All-In-One explains and models a skill and then provides focused practice, periodic review, and testing to help measure acquired skills. Progress through all skills is thorough and complete.

Grammar Rules!
GP-102 • 250 pages
Grammar Rules! is a straightforward approach to basic English grammar and English writing skills. Forty units each composed of four lessons for a total of 160 lessons, plus review, skill checks, and answers. Units build skills with Parts of Speech, Mechanics, Diagramming, and Proofreading. Solid grammar and writing skills are explained, modeled, practiced, reviewed, and tested.

Clauses & Phrases
GP-055 • 80 pages
Adverb, Adjective and Noun Clauses; Gerund, Participial and Infinitive Verbals; Gerund, Participial, Infinitive, Prepositional and Appositive Phrases.

Mechanics
GP-056 • 80 pages
Abbreviations; Apostrophes; Capitalization; Italics; Quotation Marks; Numbers; Commas; Semicolons; Colons; Hyphens; Parentheses; Dashes; Brackets; Ellipses; Slashes.

Grammar & Diagramming Sentences
GP-075 • 110 pages
The Basics; Diagramming Rules and Patterns; Nouns and Pronouns; Verbs; Modifiers; Prepositions, Conjunctions, and Special Items; Clauses and Compound-Complex Sentences.

Troublesome Grammar
GP-019 • 120 pages •
Agreement; Regular and Irregular Verbs; Modifiers; Prepositions and Case, Possessives and Contractions; Plurals; Active and Passive Voice; Comparative Forms; Word Usage; and more.

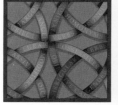